T0124200

Just a box of Souvenirs

Katreena Dayacap

authorHOUSE®

AuthorHouse™
1663 Liberty Drive
Bloomington, IN 47403
www.authorhouse.com
Phone: 1 (800) 839-8640

Published by AuthorHouse 04/22/2016

ISBN: 978-1-5246-0544-5 (sc)
ISBN: 978-1-5246-0543-8 (e)

Print information available on the last page.

Any people depicted in stock imagery provided by Thinkstock are models,
and such images are being used for illustrative purposes only.
Certain stock imagery © Thinkstock.

This book is printed on acid-free paper.

Because of the dynamic nature of the Internet, any web addresses or links contained in
this book may have changed since publication and may no longer be valid. The views
expressed in this work are solely those of the author and do not necessarily reflect the
views of the publisher, and the publisher hereby disclaims any responsibility for them.

Inspired by *You*
Written by *Me*

Introduction

This book came together by accident in all honesty. The only way I know how to savor happy moments I'd love to keep forever, was to write. I write about the heartbreak as if that person is in front of me and I'm given a chance to say exactly what the betrayal he caused, did to me. I write for the times I had no words to express the immensity of happiness I felt in love. I write for the darkness that made me stronger.

A beat

Can I follow you around
And pursue your words?
Cling to them,
As if they were your last breath
Without ever speaking.
Can I admire you from Afar?
Or maybe, just linger nearby.
Enough to be contagious,
But not close enough to catch.
Settle within your cross hairs
And target insight.
I want to find myself,
Rooted under your flesh.
So I can cultivate,
And multiply,
Then brood.
Upon the darkness in your eyes,
I am compelled to oblige
I revisit your heart from time to time.
As faint as it may seem
Deep within I find,
It still has a beat.
And possibly.
It's for me.

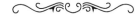

If these walls could talk
Part 1.

If these walls could talk
They would speak of
morning's sun blanketing sleeping bodies,
breakfast in bed,
And a love that swore it had no end.
They would tell of midnight dances,
Sade's serenades,
And you and I,
Hugging each other with our laughter.
If these walls spoke the truth,
They would tell of your arm
Arched over my back,
Curled like a question mark around my silence.
They would betray the secrets of sleepless nights
Of my pacing feet wearing grooves into the floor.
They would sob with the images
That covered in their corners.
Your wild eyes, and sweaty brow.
Heavy hands and painful sounds that could never be forgotten.
They would not hide the truth
Behind a broken smile
Or pack it into the backs of closets
Amidst boxes and winter coats,
only to be brought out when the weather turns cold.
If these walls could talk,
They would remind me of our story
So I could remember
How to make it end.

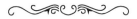

If these walls could talk.
Part II

This is a broken home
With windows and locked doors
Filled with ghost shadows and echoed voices.
Your face,
Absent from the picture frames
Yet still I see you
In the dust that lines their edges.
Your scent in my sheets
Your footsteps in the hall
I have scrubbed my skin raw
A thousand times
But find you still embedded in my pores.
Heart tomb in my chest
I have left you here to die.
Bartered emotion for sanity
And prayed for nights
When your face would no longer line the backs of eyelids.
There is no breath here.
No air.
I choke on the memory of you.
Swallow words and speak in silence.
There is nothing more to say,
Nothing left to give.
You are a cave filled up with parts of me
That I have already let go.
The gentle smile.
The beating heart.

The opened hand.
The trusting way.
All is lost,
In the aftermath of you.

I can't educate you

I can't educate you on how to fall in love.
But everything you need to know
Exists at the right bottom rim of his eyes.
I can't set the lighting,
Or tell the sky to soften the glow of the evening.
But I suggest keeping his body close as the sun sets.
Things happen when the sun sets,
Things that you can't forget
Even when it rises again.
I can't show you how to reach him, how to touch him
Or how to comfort him when he doesn't even know he needs it.
But I can tell you that when he does,
Your face should be the truest,
Your eyes should be the softest,
And your hands should tell a story across his skin.
And when the story is approaching its end
Let him reward you. He knows your deserve it.
I can't tell you how to kiss him.
But please when you do,
Kiss him like you've heard your voice for the very first time.
Like you're saving a life and making a new one,
Kiss him.
And make sure that your lips are as inviting as his quick glances
From behind the morning news.
Convince him,
That you'll never let go.
I can't tell you how to talk to him.
But remember,
Oral conversation is just as important as the exchanges
We have in silence.
The body is powerful,
Use it well.
I can't force you to share your art either.

But if you can,
Read him your journal at night.
You'll be surprised to uncover
He keeps one too.
And during those nights
When you're amidst a company of shadows,
Cling to his memory-
Attach yourself to the uncertainties
That race through his mind,
While asleep.
Rescue his heart.
His heart
That the whole time he stood before you
Hesitant to ask your name.
Sat restless,
Beating for yours.

Pages

My pages aren't blank.
Just filled with
VOID.

Para sa Mahal Ko

You flirted dangerously close
Along the lines of being everything I've ever wanted.
And when we part. your farewell,
Only means that a part of me desires you to stay.
Every time I hear your voice,
My stomach flutters with the most violent butterflies.
And I wanted to tell you my senseless rambling
Is merely nervousness.
And if I could, I would let you know
That despite all my insecurities,
I would let you explore every aspect of my being,
With hopes that you'd trust me to do the same.
How many times have I seen
Those eyes lock with mine?
You left an impression that lasted.
Gone in an instant were the memories of men
Who caught me too early in life.
Who took advantage of my romantic soul,
And present was you.
I want to memorize your voice tone,
And became so tone deaf
To only your words.
The sound of your voice
Murmuring reasons why I am exactly
What you want in life.
In you, I find refuge
To rest my exhausted soul
And throughout all my flaws,
For some unknown reason
You choose to spend every moment in my presence.
You wouldn't mind getting acquainted
With each and everything that is wrong about me
And still find ways to compliment everything right.

I wish I was your book of dreams
So you could open me,
You could erase all my mistakes
And maybe blow on me.
I want to lie in your arms,
Fingers laced with mine.
Vaguely recall caress and kiss
Hands on hips,
Moving counter clock
Lost all track of time.
Feel body half on mine.
I'm high on dreams
And I can't believe you are real.
I want to be there for you,
And that's easy
To keep the track playing on repeat,
When it's the truth.

Darkness

I fell in love with darkness
Because every time she fell,
She'd bring me to your door.
Buried in her bosom,
She handed you over willingly.
Together we leaped into the depths of her belly.
She surrounded us and for once,
Nothing else mattered.
You belonged to me.
The darkness seduced us,
She was the only garment cloaking our nakedness.
Fully exposed,
But blinded by this nighttime.
And the goose on my skin,
Were really brail.
My body's language that only your touch can comprehend.
You belonged to me,
Even if only for a little while.
I wanted to capture the darkness
And hold her hostage.
So you'd never have a reason to leave my arms.
All the shades were drawn
But I forgot about the keyholes.
I envied daylight.
Cringed as she seeped in uninvited and touched your toes.
Seductively crawling up your legs,
Warming you,
Illuminating you.
I trembled as she chased the darkness into the corners
Consuming the shadows of our passion.
You stirred in your sleep
And I attempted to clasp
The last of the darkness between our palms

Hoping it would be enough to keep you here.
But daylight smiled,
Her radiance relinquishing any remnants of us.
She took you again.
You were only mine in nighttime.
And once again,
I was forgotten like shadow puppets.
Only to be given life by darkness and your hands.

Say all that you mean

I used to think you were the end to all beings,
Tongues touch to deceive the brain
That isn't love,
Love is insane.
Now I can use all my senses except for seeing.
It's cliché to say your love blinds me.
But literally,
The wings on your back,
The flap,
the wind
and shine from the gloss on your lips.
Or maybe that's your halo
Singing melodies to the miles in me that you are running.
Pace slow,
Careful not to miss the speed bumps in my brain
Fired by nerve ending that again are paralyzed in your presence.
In other words,
I can't think when I'm near you.
I'd stop breathing just to hear you.
Speak a little louder, love the vibrations.
I'm elated at the message that you hate it.
When I smile because that means I'm not speaking
Not saying how much I miss you,
Even when you are next to me.
I'm stressed to be gratefully, lovingly, blissfully kissing you.
Dreams come true, thoughts erupt.
Not enough, wait.
Say all that you mean and even what you don't.
I never want you to leave,
I mean, no bad intentions but I'd lock you in my respiration.
Just to make sure you were the only thing I inhale.
The only sound I listen, the beat of the only drum that could ever
matter.

I know i'm imperfect,
Most super humans are.
I'm twisted in your heart strings so much that I might shatter
And if I ever get the chance at playing your strings
Know that I did the best I had.
That all this could ever mean.

Portent

Give me a moment please
I'm adjusting the roses that dance on my tongue.
I remember when I always had something to say,
But now I've lost the desire to.
Your silence is a portent to the ending of our love story.
I've become so attached to time
And ironically it makes me miss everything.
But the narcissist in you
Has caused me to stay away from what I thought I needed in the
long run.
Till this day,
I'm still recovering from our feels.
Adaptation has never been my strong point.
Where are you?
Not your physical location
But were you even with me?
All I have are these memories,
And the darkness.
The only residue of what is left,
Of us.

6 word story.

YOU GAVE HER WHAT WE HAD.

Midnight moments

Lover,
Let me lose myself in you,
Slip out of defenses
Woven into the thickness of my skin.
Drape flesh like clothes,
Slung over bedposts
And place myself before you
When midnight moments draw you in.
Lover,
Let the moonlight bare your soul.
Backbone exposed,
Let me hold your vulnerability
And trace fingertips across shoulders
That have borne the weight of your divinity.
In the night,
The skin masks no secrets
And I will wrap you in naked scars.
Embrace the wounds you wear,
For our beauty knows not of pride.
Climb inside my arms
And I will
Sink below your surface
Stitch the fabric of your frame
With the sinews of my mysteries.

Lover,
I want to lose myself in you
Cry tears of ablution
Into your chest
To heal the aching of our histories
Revive the beats of broken hearts

And remove bandages from broken bones.
Lost within your depths
And yet still
Every bit at home.

The PROMISE

You will never forget me.
My secrets,
My hair,
My laugh,
My poetry.
I'll always linger in your loneliest thoughts.
That feeling that something is missing
Will NEVER go away.
I PROMISE YOU.

I honor you

Seeking inspiration
Through the mucus membranes
Of your vocal chords.
Its vibration hits me deep.
Your name has become permanent in my everyday vocabulary.
With every swift body movement,
It personifies each punctuation mark
At the middle and ending
Of love sentences.
Your eyes illustrate perfection
As if nothing you see is negative,
Only black and white.
Repeats of a once dedicated lover.
Your lips symbolize cupids arrow
Piercing monogamous poison
Deep into the four chambers of my soul
Fascinated by the trickle of blood
That ignite the flames
Of my everyday heartburn.
The touch of your hands,
Have embraced silhouettes
Of a once entrancing mistress.
Although thoroughly cleansed
Your purity holds all truth
Of unconditional love.
As perpetual adoration.
I honor you,
"King of my heart."

Used to lay and watch you sleep,
Careful not to wake you.
I would be nervous to touch you
Because I didn't want to break anything.
Tried to figure you out.
What made you kiss me with the intensity of forever?
Only to leave.

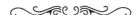

Destination

My heart awoke on my tongue
After I spoke to you last night.
It fiddled after I hummed melodies of our favorite songs
Including the one
You wrote of us,
Becomes more visible each time my cheeks swell up
Subsequent to the many compliments of how
Beautiful our seed will blossom to.
You embarked on resting your soul on my chest
While telling me burdens you've carried with you.
Shared with me the written documentaries
And songs of struggle
You wish to someday be known for.
I'll tell you this much,
I want to rip open your clothes
And memorize each beauty mark that
Lives on your skin.
So that when I practice my steady hand
Stick figures show more than lines of fallacies
But lines of pure godliness.
I want you to kiss every medium that sleeps on my body.
So that when we dream,
I can still feel your existence living on me.
And yes, it is known
That the west and the east lay on opposite sides
But we both know we're on the same map.
So I won't deter the thought of us
Will soon be when,
We partake on one of the best experiences
We would have ever asked for.

Poems titled in your name

Don't waste anymore of my time.
Give me back my secrets
And the twenty seven poems titled in your name
That I have written since we met.
And I hate that I once loved you.
That was your fault.
The dawn is still and cold
And I hate that you are happy.
Hear your laughter mingling with hers
To form a harmony like
Breeze to trees,
Thunder to wailing raindrops.
This is all wrong.
It was I who is meant to be okay if there's any justice in this world.
After all, this was all your fault.
I hate that you're okay
That you calmly answer every phone call
Where I try to pry the worst out of you
Out of this new composure you've adopted.
Your flaws is all I have ever known.
And now that you've grown,
Left me behind
I'm wondering at how wrong this has all gone.
Maybe.
It was my fault.
Maybe.
You're gone.
I've packed a box of all your stuff.
Worn shirts,
Wrapped it in all twenty seven poems.
But this time,
Your name was not used to title twenty eight.
We've come back to the mundane

And it precedes no verses.
Just your address.
I hate that I ever knew you
But I love how much I know.
Can still recognize your scent lingering around the corner.
Chased it down once when no one was looking.
Thought I heard you.
I heard wrong.
The nights are cold and restless
And I love you.
Hate that I do.
This is all wrong, and look it hurts.
But that's okay,
It was my fault.
What about me?
I swear this is the last of them.
You've probably forgotten it all already.
But I found your spare key yesterday
Thought you might come by.
In case you want it,
I won't write you anymore of these, I promise.
But remember that time
On the fire escape?
We drank Hennessey in the still dusk and laughed at how
The cold steel felt on our bare feet.
Remember that time
When you loved me?
And I was so gracefully indifferent.
It seems you loved me best
When you were but an afterthought.
That was twenty nine.
I miss you.

Outer space

Do you want to know how it feels to float in outer space?
You just need the right sound, equal in chemistry.
Without shying or straying away.
Lips mouthing out,
"I've been waiting for you to come by."
Touch.
I'm not scared to show you how you make me feel.
Connect the right dots, as I search for more spots
To let the stars glow when I reach the right rhythm
To move you out your system.
Dancing closer to the edge,
Hoping you'll fall with me
For a promise that might be.
If I get to see what type of degree that you and I can reach together.
Your lips touches mine,
Slowly I see the curves you bring out of me.
Entering my stimuli, inside your neon flux
As we suck in this cosmic dust
Into the next galaxy.
Gradually infatuated by your graphics.
Now taste you and I
And keep sharing you and me.
When kisses trade off certain sin which is pleasurable
To the highest measure.
My desire,
To take you anywhere you want to go.
If so,
Let it be Venus to share this warmth that grow between us.
Just fall into the black bottom
Where it bridges out into orange moons
Engaged with crystals.
As shooting stars send you to the climax,
Where you need to be.

To relax and take at ease,
to squeeze afterwards
With my chin breaking sweat against your forehead.
Heavy breathes match the same tempo streaming.
You and I.
Eyes closed to four,
Fingers awaken,
grasping on to sight
From the slightest touch.
Your vision still pure to me.
That even in a dream,
I'm still awake.
Willing and yearning
For the afterglow.

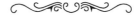

Sunshine

Lilac thoughts,
She brought sunshine to darkened rooms.
Radiating warmth upon skin
Rooted from heavens ground.
Nature's sweet caress,
You never knew how much you needed sun.

Poet

Poet,
Your words slither through my bloodstream
As if I'm addicted to
Your metaphoric infested stanzas.
Your brilliantly put phrases
Glisten behind boastful eyes.
Reading through the cracks of my inner bosom,
You reflect my past as if you knew me.
I linger on your every word
Because it all makes sense.
If your words could jump off the page
And into my hands
I would embrace them with the tips of my tongue
Only enough to taste your inner spirit.
And if so,
Your words would truly become my story.
Poet,
I've longed for someone to touch me this deep.
Longed for someone to strip me naked and reveal my flesh.
Because under my skin,
The scars never seem to surface.
They never made it out to breathe for air.
My scars never had the chance to heal,
Until your words anointed them.
Your medicine has my heart beating
A thousand miles an hour.
Tachycardia might be the death of me.
But let me die
Because i'm ready to be a chapter in your story.
Poet,
Your words reflect my prayers.
Answering them as if you were God himself.
You are my calling.

Sometimes i tend to believe
That you are unreal.
I tend to believe that the blood
That pours out of my skin
Are already created into words.
So that all you have to do is stamp your paper.
And your heartfelt emotions
Will permanently stay.
I love reading you,
Hearing you,
Wanting you,
Poet.

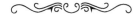

Dying butterflies

He killed what i have left.
Now there's nothing.
Not even an ounce of compassion left.
The butterflies,
Slowly dying.
The wings that once fluttered so wildly,
Are now no more.
I can hardly feel them beat.
My heart stolen,
Only to be returned, tattered and half broken.
Because he can't hurt me anymore, not completely.
Idiotic attempts at being "just friends."
Redundant.
I can't run from my emotions
Even if he can.
I'm not the type to be ignored and dropped
Only to acknowledged and picked up when he see's fit.
All this compassion now from your end?
For what?
I thought we had no chemistry.
Or is it that since i'm no longer yours,
That you're scared.
Scared that someone else is going to pick up where you left off
And show me that i am worthy to be loved.
But you need to know so much
And kisses when you want cause you "care."
He can't figure me out
So he runs to her because he knows all about her
Off a three day connection?

Bullshit.
I used to ask myself, "why can't he love me?"
And now I realize, he's afraid to love me
Because I'm the challenge he can't beat.

Jane and Tarzan

I'm mentally crushing on this man of words.
An Original poet who creatively turns six senses into
Adjectives, metaphors and adverbs.
I follow his wisdom literally by every letter.
Like a perfectionist who's down on himself
Only to become better.
It seems like he makes love to his poetry.
I'd dream of being his journal book,
So he can open me,
He could erase all my mistakes and maybe blow on me.
Diminishing words that were never meant to be.
I'd be longing for the moments he'd retrace his steps.
Molding my simplicity into greater depths.
He doesn't know that i could be
The air that he breathes.
Like air,
I'm unnoticed but a necessity.
It's hurting me
Like wooden splinters on bare feet.
Like Goliath's unruly defeat
My chance at us being one lands as great as his fall.
But as long as i read his threads
My hopes still stand tall.
It's because of him my interest for poetry has grown.
Maybe he and i will unite,
'Til then i'll stay unknown.
I love that i have a lot to learn,
I'd love him as a teacher.
Maybe love would them blossom
Like Jane and her pupil,
Tarzan didn't know much either.
So my secret poet,

Because of your words
I strive to be better.
And maybe then you and I
Can create beautiful words together.

When you loved me

Asked you to stay the night
Too late to drive so far.
I said
Had your safety in mind
Surprised when you said yes
The way you did mumbling something about winter in the city and
snow.
I shrugged.
Too tired to discuss
Offered you the couch
Hoping you'd take the bed.
Surprised when you did.
Now I lay in arms that smell familiar.
Fingers laced with mine
Can count your breath on my eyelids
Vaguely recall caress and kiss
Hands on hips
Moving counter clock
Lost all track of timed
Feel body half on mine.
I'm high on dreams
Didn't know you were real
Until your scent found my pillow
Rolled over,
Saw your face.
Just to the right of my everything,
Fingertips brush lips
Dance across cheeks
Don't remember your breath so steady
Don't remember your skin so soft
Don't remember loving you this much.
You,
So beautiful and calm in sleep.

I,
Restless, want to steal your peace
Make it mine
Like you should be.
Vaguely recall caress and kiss
Hands on hips
Now feel arm around waist
Pull me close.
Knees find thighs
Nose find place where shoulder meets neck.
Feel my breath on your eyelids.
Find my scent,.
Watch my name escape as whisper.
Exist as dance.
Across cheeks.
Brush lips,
Breath steady,
Skin so soft.
Don't remember loving you this much,
Can barely breath now from holding air.
Can't move
Can't let you.
High on dreams.
Me,
Lost in memory.
Remembering when you and I,
Were we.
Were us.
Were meant to be.
Breath so steady
Skin so soft.
Remembering when you loved me
This much.

Broken

Today,
I let you go.
Untangled my fingers from your ribs,
Your mouth from my ears
And my heart from your soul.
I left you broken.
Don't look back to see
The catastrophe I had caused.
Cause,
I had already turned to stone.
Cold.
Muscle no longer stiff,
I ripped myself away from you
With no warning.
Withdrew,
To leave you with the hurting
That you gave to me.
I scraped rug burns on your knees,
Callous on your hands,
Lies in your eyes
And insecurities in your heart.
Ripped apart emotions
Then gave them back as tokens
Of my fake apologies.
You believed me.
And I laughed at you.
So foolish to believe,
That you had me wrapped so tight around your finger.
That I would still linger,
After you dismembered our affection.
I'm guessing you thought my tears were erosions
Creating a new path for you and I.
But they were the beginning of oceans

That drowned out our dreams
And opened up paths to deceit.
Revenge took over me,
You were so open to me.
So,
I lied to you.
Hurt you,
Broke you,
Over again and again,
And when i heard karma knocking on my door,
I let you go.
Freed you from this rapture
Of hate hiding between my fingers
Ready to wrap around your throat
And choke the happiness from your soul.
I let you go.
And we both remained,
Broken.

I have known you all along

Still i am reminded of the moment we met
And the only sight that could ever contend to be as beautiful
Was the vision of you walking away because
Us parting meant that we were once connected,
And what could be as beautiful as that.
A bittersweet picture
Forced inside a regretful frame of mind
And i am reminded.
You told me i was everything you ever wanted
And maybe the reason i pushed you away is because
I was terribly frightened
At even the mere thought of being that close
To eternity,
I could almost touch it.
I never told you but
Thousands of years before we were formally introduced
I had already considered spending
The rest of my lives with you.
Yes,
I past times i knew.
I watched you from afar
As you played your guitar;
Swayed with the crowd making occasional eye contact
Hoping you would notice
But you never broke your focus.
And in faraway lands
I was the sand beneath your feet.
Even then i adored you,
And although we had yet to meet.
I was reminded of every word you ever said to me.
The only thing that ever came close
To sounding as sweet
Was the tone of your voice

As you whispered goodbye to me
Because your difficult farewell
Only means that parts of you desired to stay.
Maybe the reason i pushed you away
Is because i was terribly frightened
At even the mere thought of
Being that close to eternity
I could almost touch it.
I never told you
but the first night you said you loved me
I looked into your eyes and i swear,
I saw forever staring back at me.
The air reeked of fear.
And the only thing that frightened me to that degree
Was the idea of you leaving and never coming back.
It reminds me of the moment we met
And suddenly i am no longer afraid of touching eternity.
You told me that it was the only possible way you could ever stay.
"I do."
And you'll never believe me but
I have known it all along.

Love wounds

He-
Slips and slides past tissue,
Wiping stains on sheets.
We bend and fold into positions,
Kissing old wounds
And inflicting love scars.
Bite marks.
Territorial scratches on backs.
Our passion flowing down cracks
And swallowed
On the tips of our tongues.
I whisper i love-
And he bites my tongue,
Sucks my lips
And tries to push away emotions.
Even though i've been hoping
We'd share more than fluids.
Been wanting to make it exclusive but,
He was only mine to borrow.
Until now.
Folded in the creases of my heart,
Blossoming in my soul.
Beginning to grow
Past my ribs and tangling
With the strings attached to my heart.
I'm weakening with each thrust.
He's breaking down barriers
While tearing flesh.
Less ego, more sincerity.
He stares at me and i fall into the moment.
You got me.
His stroking, then holding me
Cause my legs won't stop shaking,

These walls won't stop breaking
And i'm becoming submissive.
Giving him all of me,
Pushing past knees, digging deep
Trying to reach me.
Then,
Somewhere between
He explodes.
Minor earthquakes take place.
After shocks made the levees break
And he drowns in me.
Love.
Submerged under my skin.
He takes existence in my thoughts
Buries himself in my memory
To be sure i never forget him.
Then, with no warning
Everything we just built becomes so broken.
Now scattered across the room,
He moved too quickly for the door
Before i could tell him
He had my heart-
Stolen.
It just doesn't make sense.
He whispered he loves and-
I assumed.
I assumed the words that would follow would be me.
I assumed-
This moment was so much more than fucking.
But we've never been anything more
Than passion tangled with lust,
Confusing it with love.

Carbon copy

Excuse me.
But would i be out of line
If i asked for an illustration,
A print,
Or better yet,
A complete carbon copy of
You?
Not literally but everything that makes
Well.
You.
Personality, compassion, insight,
Foresight, structure, style
And most importantly, your mind.
At worst, just trace an outline
Or design a paint-by-numbers scheme
For me to map out your every thought
So i may place them among my fantasies.
If i could,
I would record your voice
And create playlists of your melodic vocals
Set always on repeat.
Transcending the limits
For which my eardrums can register
Beauty at its purest.
I know this request is quite a bit out of the ordinary
But don't waste a single breath of my person.
For i am truly not worthy
To be graced by the original.
For too long i've remained frozen,
Unplaced with another to call myself equivalent
Yet i admit it's okay to sleep because
You see,
You could be what turns my nightmares

Into daydreams.
And i think if even just a piece of you,
Gently pressed between laminae
Bound between my serenity
Would be more than enough
To satisfy my every emotion
Even if you could spare
An illustration, a print
... or better yet,
A complete carbon copy
Of you.

Measure your height

Surgical incisions, outlined in temporary shades.
Times change,
Thus beauty strays from your tired soul
So i capture your awkward balance of life and sleep
In my photographic memory box labeled
This is how i dream.
Eyes?
They wander.
Love,
To places they don't belong.
Smiles?
They hand out kisses to faces washed with dirty palms.
I never argued my part,
So won't you listen to me now.
New bodies write new stories
About princesses and fairytales.
My old soul is loving your new ways.
When you laughed at your simple flaws
When the mirror didn't tell you how beautiful you are
I remember being bound to brown corneas.
Now i've drowned in blue waves
Of discolored astigmatism.
And those waves spill over into my cupped hands
Saving the thirst for the day that your tongue dries
For the air you've been breathing
For someone else.
Feet?
They walk all over the faithful.
You know, leaving imprints for lasting losses.
Hearts?
They break when stepped on.
Love,
Your one shoe size too heavy.

You've weighed yourself down to the thinnest layer
Stripping fashion crazes,
Unclothed to modest beliefs.
Stunting mind growth
By drinking pop culture cappuccinos.
Entering another life form
Quick to leave yourself behind.
But i'm here to paint your picture
With cosmetic smears around your aura.
I never did argue my part,
But you ought to measure your height
Because you're quite a tall tale.

All because of you

Keeping my demeanor well composed,
I sit.
Eyes blank.
Emotionless but tear filled.
My silence spoke volumes that reached your soul
Almost like a ball of anguish,
And it's all because of you.
your actions both thoughtless and selfish caused damage
Shattering what was left of our perfect picture.
My expression says,
There's nothing left to salvage.
Our love is done and it's all because of you.
Although guilt stricken,
It is I who you want to console.
Want me to caress your ego with words of forgiveness.
But the vibe i have for you is defeated and cold.
I am torn,
And it's all because of you.
"I'm sorry," he mutters what he genuinely felt.
He allowed himself to give into his bodies craving
Forgetting everything we've worked for and built.
Ruined.
Tears streaked my face, past lips.
They parted and i said no louder than a whisper,
"Your actions proved we are nothing.
and it hurts me to say,
i will miss you.
But you've ruined what has took so long to build.
I jumped through hoops to be what you wanted me to be.

I fought for your heart.
Do you know,
You made me want to have you forever.
But you slept when i fell in love."

So i wrote to bring him closer

So i wrote to bring him closer
From where we last fell off.
On the bandwagon making sharp u-turns
Sliding on slopes made slippery when wet.
So i wrote to adversely change his yesterday.
With adverbs that allowed room for expansion.
When we're 48, we will have this conversation.
We will discuss our exchanges with other people
And the lessons we have never learned well enough.
And i promise that we will both attempt to make a go of this again
But i will refuse.
However, this is not the time.
So take the umbrella as you leave
Because it's storming outside,
And i have much to pen down before it leaves my mind state
In a mix of random thoughts-
Yet again.
So let me write to bring you closer
To push you far enough
Just to be noticed from the coffee shop down the street
Mutually accept the smile and always intend to stop
Fully aware that the weather will always be in-climate
And you will always forget the umbrella
And get caught in the rain.

Better than you

All you readers can say this piece sucks
But it prevents me from writing poems like,
"I miss your breath on my neck, arousing each tiny hair
That sends pulses to my heart, can't breathe without you" poems
"I will be better poems,
I want to be with you even though you cheated" poems.
If this bitter, egotistical, riding a high horse,
Self aware, cocky poem is what it takes to get over you
I will write away and still
Be better than you.

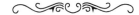

Dear God

Dear God,
One-
I have stopped beating myself up on where my actions will send me.
Two-
I don't believe in hell.
Three-
And if it does exist,
Unconditional love does not.
Four-
If you love me,
Love me dirty, filled with flaws.
After all,
It was you, who told me I could never be perfect,
So why try and make me pretend.
Five-
Please don't perceive me as ornery or contrary.
I just don't understand.
Six-
How do you know I will never reach perfection?
But you ask to practice?
Or how you love me unconditionally but won't accept me.
Seven-
I didn't ask to find his kisses so relieving.
Or his eyes so beautiful...
Eight-
I never wanted to feel this way.
Nine-
Everyone says that I am going to hell.
And I must admit,
I'm scared.
Ten-
If I pretend,
Will you accept me?

Will I be worthy of the taking
For being so obedient.
For relinquishing my happiness to walk next to him?
To procreate?
Eleven-
You gave your only begotten son,
I should be more than willing to give up
"My sins."
Twelve-
I know you are not waiting,
And I maybe late
But I'm just not ready.
P.S.
I love you.

Snowflakes

Born on front steps
Between a lover and a muse
And to this day,
I can't erase that mental image of you.
Upside down,
Across your lap, hands clasp
As snowflakes fall late before their summer nap.
I never knew not in that moment
When I gave you my heart
That I would miss it so much.
Long to hear it beating in my chest
To warm my soul
Make me feel alive again at best.
How can you possess so many and still be heartless?
Cold truth has crept up my spine
And fallen neatly over my mind.
Not unlike those snowflakes
Scattering the otherwise perfect start to my demise
And I finally, half heartedly realize
You are not, and never will be mine.
I wait for this to fall apart
For you to break me in two
I know where this is going
And I tell myself to turn back
And the strength falls,
As do I.
Use me, I like it.
Take me for granted.
You've ripped my heart out it will not get any worse than this.
What do I have to lose?
The way I see it, all I am risking is you.
Here I am, ready to give in.
A clouded conscience comes to mind

Screaming in covered ears
Telling me what I knowingly ignore
I don't want to hear!
I'm aware.
Tears fall frantically,
Grasp for air,
Praying mercilessly.
Can't let go.
I can't handle this affliction
Addiction.
You are my sick fix.

Not feeling very creative

I'm not feeling very creative but this I have to say
Hate the way you played with me,
Laid with me,
And laughed right in my face.
Ripped out my heart,
Took a bite and put it on display
Told all my friends and foes
I was a girl that could be played.
And still, I'm not feeling very creative but.
Did you enjoy yourself?
Have fun when you sucked out my soul
Price tagged it, shelved it
Discounted me you sold.
Marked me down, red tag event
My soul must have been old.
Damaged maybe,
Dropped and kicked
The band-aid patch you used to renew
Showed too bright and bold.
I'm still not feeling very creative
But I'm sure you did when you broke my heart
Then paper matched it back together
Just to see if it would look the same,
Love the same,
Then you did me one better.
Hot glued back in my broken soul
Because you liked getting your fingers dirty.
And to see me withdrew and hurting.
And I wasn't feeling very creative
But I remember
Trying to glue laces and glitter to my heart
So it would be more attractive to you
But you weren't too fond of my antics

And my heart you threw away with old photographs of me
When I was happy
But now it's just a lonely night.
You left me-
Palms to the lord,
Praying I could be as creative as you.
Asked him to inspire me
And take my hands
And make a mess out of you.
Dig my hands into your heart
So I can feel alive again
Be creative again
Because you tell me creativity is under the skin
And you love to watch your creations bleed.
Yes I know why I'm not feeling it
Creativity out the door.
Because you chain sawed open my cranium,
Cracked open my chest cavity
And in your attempt to fix me,
You left part of my cerebellum on the floor

Waves

My soul's language is floral,
Deeply rooted in flesh.
Hunger for love
That is deep, undiscovered and mysterious,
I crave the oceans kiss.

 Where I want to go

I see the moon in your eyes.
You know,
I'm not very different from you.
There's a burning desire in me
That wants to touch things deeper,
A place where hands are not invited.
Soul energy.
I live for the chance to experience that.

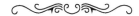

Rose child

Protect me from all evil,
And banish the negativity that can easily find its way.
I am the rose child
Among the universes garden.
Maintaining happiness,
I yearn for the moons healing energy.

Experience induced poetry

Immaturity grows
Into experience induced poetry.
You introduced me to more than underground artists,
Produced a palate of visions I otherwise,
Would have never seen for myself.
Expanded my horizons
In a time when all I saw was
Vertical stagnation.
Grabbed me by the hand,
In response my mind reacted
Took the physical to another level,
We are chemically infused.
I considered you an inspiration chaser
Ran without hesitation
As soon as I knew you wanted to meet me halfway.
Paper thin layers,
I'm still yearning to accustom my body.
Adaptation has never been my strong point.
When you left, or rather I
It was then when I covered my palms
With gloves of in destruction.
Constantly trying to recapture an expression
Far too long ago versed.
Words don't hold the same weight
Without your head resting.
I feel my fingers itching to dial
A memorized combination of numerals.
Your voice alters my ability to create.
In a way unthinkable,
Perhaps that's why you always referred to yourself as original.
Started off at the same point together
Drifted off towards separate directions,
After the scribbles and crumples,

You're the first and only to describe me perfectly.
Embrace my growth, leaps and downfalls unconditionally.
Because you cared at the moments where I could barely hold a pen,
Let alone anyone else's hands but yours.
...Oh, but the way your mouth moves against mine,
Indulgence taken to the 9th level in clouds,
Painted on the deepest blue
Matching the eyes that are piercing right through
The weakened knees of my soul.
Resistance,
Nonexistent.
Exhuming every desire from my depths to be displayed
For your eyes only.
Your hand caresses my face,
Moving me like the sweetest of love poems
And I fall into you
As you sink to my level.
The pain of it
Keeping me on the very brink of reality.
A reminder that-
This cannot last forever.
The praise of your kisses,
The tenderness in your touch.
I move underneath you trembling, it is almost too much.
Sorrow swept into the corners of my eyes
To be wiped away thoughtlessly,
You changed my life.
Your eyes wash over me
Leaving me feeling beautiful and exposed
The beauty of your body.
Breath caught in my throat
As you too off your clothes
Then ever so gently removed mine.
I have never wanted anyone so badly in my life.
But you just held me
Telling me stories with adoring eyes
And cherishing lips of the lightest kiss on my forehead
And hands.

Never taking advantage,
Only giving bliss.
I love you for that.
This right here,
This is addiction.
I just wanted you to hold me
Ease the self-conscious state that I live in.
Disappointment followed by
Routine aching throbs in the back of my throat
Somewhere between vomit and a scream,
Moans of agony escaping my lungs
You move quicker,
Mistaking pain for love.
Another hole,
There is no me.
Single syllables of four letters,
Fall on the cracks in my ego,
Expanding the ever-growing gap in my chest.
Old sutures tremble,
Head turned to the left
I like the filth of it all.
Makes me feel wanted,
Sort of needed at least.
But in the wake of this moment
Contemplating what's lost
I feel violation creep up my spine.
Draining remnants of pride from my mind,
Eternally broken
I lay in the stains
Wrapped in a blanket,
Only a shell remains.

Seasons

Hopefully,
One day you'll chase my imagination
While letting yours run free
And let the feeling drip slowly
As I reflect
And I lay back and take you in.
I'll take you in quietly
And still pray that newness won't end.
And I know, it's far too fresh
In our season to say
That this is love.
But between you and I,
I think you unintentionally
Give me something like that
Spring summer feeling.

The ending.

I loved you before I saw your real face.

X-rays

Mirrors.
I hate them.
Always reflecting lies.
I prefer x-rays,
Show me what's inside.
Show me your heart,
Something I can relate to
Both torn and misused.
We get caught up being locked out
Never going deeper than the surface.
Our focus,
Only skin.
Though some aim for blood.
But what about the brain?
What about the small veins so close to the spine
Sending signals to your mind.
I want to know them.
I want our signals to connect
But so much more than physical
Because your skin means nothing to me.
Merely just a box casing your soul
And promoting insecurities.
Let me read your memories
So I know where you've been.
And assist you where you want to go.
Let's grow separate, but close.
Feeding off each other enough
So it's not detrimental.
Love should first be spiritual
Before you even get physical
Because anything physical
Is bound to be abused.
And let's get used to just hearing each other speak.

Miscommunication is what can make us weak
Plus your words and feelings is of value to me.
I'm sure you think these are just words.
Empty.
But I can only show you,
Not like mirrors.
Like X-rays.
So you can see through the outside,
Inside.
Where it really matters.

I hope you're happy
With this new found path you've created for yourself.
You've mistaken routine for comfort,
You've escaped past mistakes to make future ones.

HIM

Reality is,
I couldn't turn him into a husband.
And the truth is,
I can't become accustom to the child and all the women.
It just doesn't set right,
And it's not the business.
The real deal is,
At some point in life, I'd like to be a wife
And not a slant route.
I'd like to know that I came first
And not seventh.
And when I'm pregnant,
I don't want four other women to be mad at me for it.
I want a pot belly and a man to adore it
And show up at four in the morning with hot tea and roses
Because I can't sleep.
I want a man that doesn't creep,
I need a dude that puts me in the mood
To fly to the moon
And he'll want to hear all about it when I get back.
He wouldn't go because he'd let me be independent.
And while I'd be walking on blue cheese,
He'd be at home on his knees praying for my safe return.
That's the kind of man I want.
And I desire the heart of a thousand raging fires
When he touches my breasts and thighs
And I won't have to wonder
why he'll smell like perfume because the scent
I'll pick up on him will always be mine.
I'll define greatness,
And he'll mirror me as my equal.

He'll encourage my laugher and wipe away tears
And let me run camp and quiet my fears.
I'll cook him elaborate dinners
And sex him crazy passionate.
I'll encourage all his dreams
And I'll be the one he'll share them with.
See,
Even after all the heartache and poor choices,
I still believe in love.
I believe that something other
than what I've chosen for myself exists
And I'll find it at the right moment.
I feel his energy on me now.
He'll be single, tall and hardworking.
He'll be creative and loving.
He'll adore each inch of me and respect the ground I walk on
And admire the radius of my aura that stretch for miles around me.
What others were blind to see,
He'll see.
He won't make me wonder where he's been all weekend
And his intentions will be nothing less than genuine.
He'll hold me in the highest esteem
And not seem like the one-
He'll actually be him,
When I meet him,
I'll be done writing these things that confuse old lovers
And anger new ones on the scene.
I'll be done pinning over perpetrators
And forever dismiss the men that didn't take the time to really get to
know me.
Gone will be the hazy days
And broken will be that long strand of time
I spent caught in the maze
Thinking I deserved less.
I'm a whole woman
Who needs more than half a man.

When he's ready to stand by my side
And turn this hell into a life.
I'll look him in the eye,
Nod quietly,
And give him my outstretched hand.

About the Author

Katreena has been writing poetry for about 16 years already and she's been doing a lot of open mic to spoken word poetry. She happily lives in Rhode Island.

Printed in the United States
By Bookmasters